About The Founder

Altimese Nichole is an author, speaker, brand strategist, and publicist, with a heart to help her clients win. She attained her undergraduate degree in Mass Communications, Broadcast Journalism from Virginia Commonwealth University and completed her Master of Management degree from the University of Phoenix

Altimese is a former director of social media in Corporate America-- turned agency owner after an unexpected layoff. After a difficult season in her life, she discovered the meaning of EZER K'Negdo and made it her mission to live her truth boldly while inspiring all women to do the same. Through adversity, The Ezer Agency was born.

Altimese has over 12 years of experience with big brand marketing, including CNN, Cartoon Network, Black Bride Magazine, Church's Chicken, Sutter Home Wines, and more.

Learn more about Altimese Nichole at www.altimesenichole.com.

About The Ezer Agency

BRILLIANT STRATEGY. SMART EXECUTION.

The Ezer Agency is the HELP Agency. We help our clients and partners to showcase their brand story to their ideal customer through strategic, powerful storytelling.

EZER derives from the Hebrew language. It can accompany the modifier, K'Negdo/Kenegdo- to reflect Ezer K'Negdo/Kenegdo.

It comes from two root words meaning "to rescue, to save" and "to be strong" (R. David Freedman, "Woman, a Power Equal to Man").

Ezer consults.
Ezer delivers.
Ezer gets it done.

Ezer HELPS YOU DISCOVER THE POWER OF YOUR BRAND'S STORY

Copyright © 2021 by Altimese Nichole Enterprise, LLC.

All rights reserved. No part of this publication may be reproduced, distributed, or transmitted in any form or by any means, including photocopying, recording, or other electronic or mechanical methods, without the prior written permission of the publisher, except in the case of brief quotations embodied in critical reviews and certain other noncommercial uses permitted by copyright law. For permission requests, write to the publisher, addressed "Attention: Permissions Coordinator," at the address below.

Altimese Nichole Entperprise, LLC DBA The Ezer Agency
PO Box 2002
Savannah, GA 31402

Printed by Altimese Nichole Enterprise, LLC, in the United States of America.

Front cover image by The Ezer Agency
Book design by The Ezer Agency

www.theezeragency.com

Yearly Goals

Main Goals

Main Goal 01 Steps   Status   Due Date

Main Goal 02 Steps   Status   Due Date

Main Goal 03 Steps   Status   Due Date

Action Plans

1.
2.
3.
4.
5.
6.
7.
8.
9.
10.
11.
12.
13.
14.
15.
16.

Notes

Marketing Plan

SMART Goals

Specific	Measurable	Achievable	Relevent	Timeframe

Marketing Objectives | KPI's

Core Audience(s) | Additional Notes

Username & Passwords

Platform/Website	Username	Password

Media Spend Tracker

Month	Approved Budget	Amount Spent	Remaining/Overage
JAN			
FEB			
MAR			
APR			
MAY			
JUNE			
JULY			
AUG			
SEP			
OCT			
NOV			
DEC			

Notes:

Business Contact List

Name
Job Title
Email
Phone no.

Name
Job Title
Email
Phone no.

Name
Job Title
Email
Phone no.

Name
Job Title
Email
Phone no.

Name
Job Title
Email
Phone no.

Name
Job Title
Email
Phone no.

Name
Job Title
Email
Phone no.

Name
Job Title
Email
Phone no.

Name
Job Title
Email
Phone no.

Name
Job Title
Email
Phone no.

Name
Job Title
Email
Phone no.

Name
Job Title
Email
Phone no.

January

Year 2021

"Think like a queen. A queen is not afraid to fail. Failure is another stepping stone to greatness."
– Oprah Winfrey

Monthly And Daily Socially Relevant Holidays

Themes for the month of January:

- Financial Wellness Month
- Get A Balanced Life Month
- Get Organized Month
- International Creativity Month
- International New Years Resolutions Month for Businesses
- International Wealth Mentality Month
- National Be On-Purpose Month
- National Mentoring Month
- National Slavery and Human Trafficking Prevention Month

Monthly And Daily Socially Relevant Holidays

January 2021 hashtag calendar:

- January 1 – New Year's Day #NewYearsDay
- January 2 – National Motivation and Inspiration Day #MotivationandInspirationDay
- January 2 – Science Fiction Day #ScienceFictionDay
- Januar 2 – World Introvert Day #WorldIntrovertDay
- January 4 – National Trivia Day #NationalTriviaDay
- January 6 – National Technology Day #NationalTechnologyDay
- January – National Vision Board Day #VisionBoardDay
- January 11 – Human Trafficking Awareness Day #HumanTraffickingAwarenessDay
- January 11 – Clean Off Your Desk Day #CleanOffYourDeskDay
- January 13 – National Sticker Day #NationalStickerDay
- January 13 – Public Radio Broadcasting Day #PublicRadioBroadcastingDay
- January 14 – Organize Your Home Day #OrganizeYourHomeDay
- January 15 – Humanitarian Day #HumanitarianDay
- January 15 – National Hat Day #NationalHatDay
- January 16 – Get to Know Your Customers Day #GetToKnowYourCustomersDay
- January 20 – Martin Luther King Jr. Day #MLKDay
- January 21 – National Hugging Day #NationalHuggingDay
- January 23 – National Pie Day #PieDay
- January 24 – National Compliment Day #NationalComplimentDay
- January 25 – Chinese New Year #YearOfTheRat
- January 25 – Opposite Day #OppositeDay
- January 27 – Community Manager Appreciation Day #CMAD
- January 31 – Backwards Day #BackwardsDay

Calender

Monday	Tuesday	Wednesday	Thursday	Friday	Saturday	Sunday
28	29	30	31	1	2	3
4	5	6	7	8	9	10
11	12	13	14	15	16	17
18	19	20	21	22	23	24
25	26	27	28	29	30	31

Notes

www.theezeragency.com

Content Strategy

Facebook

Account Name
Post Frequency
Content Ideas

Goals

Twitter

Account Name
Post Frequency
Content Ideas

Goals

Instagram

Account Name
Post Frequency
Content Ideas

Goals

Pinterest

Account Name
Post Frequency
Content Ideas

Goals

Media	No. of Subscribers	No. of Sales
Facebook		
Twitter		
Pinterest		
Instagram		

Blog Status

Notes

Monthly Paid Media Budget

Platform	Objective	Approved Budget
Total		

Audience Details

Platform:

Total expenses

Notes

Blog Post Monthly

Blog theme _____ **Month of** _____

Day	Title	Category	Done

Notes

The Blog Post

PUBLISH DATE	CATEGORY	POST TYPE
POST TITLE		
RELATED SERIES		

Blog Notes

Description

- ....
- ....
- ....
- ....
- ....

Key Points

- ....
- ....
- ....
- ....
- ....

Input Links

- ....
- ....
- ....

Social Media

☐ f ☐ 📷 ☐ P

Output Links

- ....
- ....
- ....

SPONSORS

GIVEAWAYS

FREEBIES

Notes

The Blog Post

| PUBLISH DATE | CATEGORY | POST TYPE |

POST TITLE

RELATED SERIES

BLOG NOTES

DESCRIPTION

-
-
-
-
-

KEY POINTS

-
-
-
-
-

INPUT LINKS

-
-
-

SOCIAL MEDIA

☐ f ☐ 📷 ☐ P

OUTPUT LINKS

-
-
-

SPONSORS

GIVEAWAYS

FREEBIES

NOTES

The Blog Post

PUBLISH DATE	CATEGORY	POST TYPE
POST TITLE		
RELATED SERIES		

Blog Notes

Description

- ....
- ....
- ....
- ....
- ....
- ....

Key Points

- ....
- ....
- ....
- ....
- ....
- ....

Input Links

- ....
- ....
- ....

Social Media

☐ f ☐ ⊙ ☐ p

Output Links

- ....
- ....
- ....

SPONSORS

GIVEAWAYS

FREEBIES

Notes

The Blog Post

PUBLISH DATE	CATEGORY	POST TYPE
POST TITLE		
RELATED SERIES		

BLOG NOTES

DESCRIPTION

- [ ] ....
- [ ] ....
- [ ] ....
- [ ] ....
- [ ] ....

KEY POINTS

- [ ] ....
- [ ] ....
- [ ] ....
- [ ] ....
- [ ] ....

INPUT LINKS

- [ ] ....
- [ ] ....
- [ ] ....

SOCIAL MEDIA

- [ ] **f**   - [ ] 📷   - [ ] ▢   - [ ] **p**

OUTPUT LINKS

- [ ] ....
- [ ] ....
- [ ] ....

SPONSORS

GIVEAWAYS

FREEBIES

NOTES

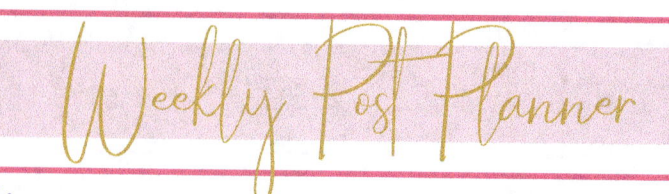

WEEK OF:

- DATE:
- BLOG TITLE:
- IDEAS:
- TAGS:
- CATEGORIES:
- KEYWORD PHRASE:
- CALL TO ACTION:
- AFFILIATE LINK TO PROMOTE:

TO DO:

POST PROMOTION:

WEEK OF:

- DATE:
- BLOG TITLE:
- IDEAS:
- TAGS:
- CATEGORIES:
- KEYWORD PHRASE:
- CALL TO ACTION:
- AFFILIATE LINK TO PROMOTE:

TO DO:

POST PROMOTION:

WEEK OF:

- DATE:
- BLOG TITLE:
- IDEAS:
- TAGS:
- CATEGORIES:
- KEYWORD PHRASE:
- CALL TO ACTION:
- AFFILIATE LINK TO PROMOTE:

TO DO:

POST PROMOTION:

Weekly Post Planner

WEEK OF:

- DATE:
- BLOG TITLE:
- IDEAS:
- TAGS:
- CATEGORIES:
- KEYWORD PHRASE:
- CALL TO ACTION:
- AFFILIATE LINK TO PROMOTE:

TO DO:

POST PROMOTION:

WEEK OF:

- DATE:
- BLOG TITLE:
- IDEAS:
- TAGS:
- CATEGORIES:
- KEYWORD PHRASE:
- CALL TO ACTION:
- AFFILIATE LINK TO PROMOTE:

TO DO:

POST PROMOTION:

WEEK OF:

- DATE:
- BLOG TITLE:
- IDEAS:
- TAGS:
- CATEGORIES:
- KEYWORD PHRASE:
- CALL TO ACTION:
- AFFILIATE LINK TO PROMOTE:

TO DO:

POST PROMOTION:

Analytics

Total Users:

New Users:

Page Views

Bounce Rate

| 1 | 2 | 3 | 4 | 5 | 6 | 7 | 8 | 9 | 10 | 11 | 12 |

Pinterest Followers

Pinterest Monthly Views

Email Subscribers

New Subscribers

Instagram Followers

Twitter Followers

Facebook Page Likes

Facebook Group Members

Notes:

Community Management

Outreach Notes

M	T	W	T	F	S
☐	☐	☐	☐	☐	☐
☐	☐	☐	☐	☐	☐
☐	☐	☐	☐	☐	☐
☐	☐	☐	☐	☐	☐
☐	☐	☐	☐	☐	☐
☐	☐	☐	☐	☐	☐
☐	☐	☐	☐	☐	☐
☐	☐	☐	☐	☐	☐
☐	☐	☐	☐	☐	☐
☐	☐	☐	☐	☐	☐
☐	☐	☐	☐	☐	☐
☐	☐	☐	☐	☐	☐

Notes

February

Year 2021

> "I didn't get there by wishing for it or hoping for it, but by working for it."
> – Estée Lauder

Monthly And Daily Socially Relevant Holidays

Themes for the month of February:

- African-American Cultural Heritage Month
- American Heart Month
- International Month of Black Women in The Arts
- National Black History Month
- National Time Management Month
- National Weddings Month
- National Women Inventors Month
- North American Inclusion Month (NAIM)

Weeks of observance in February:

- International Networking Week: February 1-5
- African Heritage & Health Week: February 1-7
- Women's Heart Week: February 1-7
- American Association for The Advancement of Science Week: February 8-11
- Freelance Writer Appreciation Week: February 8-13
- Random Acts of Kindness Week: February 8-14
- National Entrepreneurship Week: February 13-20

Monthly And Daily Socially Relevant Holidays

February 2021 hashtag calendar:

- February 2 – Groundhog Day #GroundhogDay
- February 2 – World Wetlands Day #WorldWetlandsDay
- February 4 – World Cancer Day #WorldCancerDay
- February 5 – National Weatherperson's Day #NationalWeatherpersonsDay
- February 5 – National Bubble Gum Day #BubbleGumDay
- February 7 – Super Bowl LV #SuperBowl2021
- February 7 – National Send a Card to a Friend Day #SendACardToAFriendDay
- February 8 – National Boy Scouts Day #BoyScoutsDay
- February 9 – National Pizza Day #NationalPizzaDay
- February 11 – Safer Internet Day #SID2021
- February 11 – Inventors Day #InventorsDay
- February 13 – Self-Love Day #SelfLoveDay
- February 13 – World Radio Day #WorldRadioDay
- February 14 – Valentine's Day #ValentinesDay
- February 14 – International Book Giving Day #InternationalBookGivingDay
- February 15 – Presidents Day #PresidentsDay
- February 16 – Mardi Gras #MardiGras
- February 17 – Random Acts of Kindness Day #RandomActsOfKindnessDay
- February 18 – National Battery Day #NationalBatteryDay
- February 20 – World Day of Social Justice #SocialJusticeDay
- February 20 – Love Your Pet Day #LoveYourPetDay
- February 21 – International Mother Language Day #IMLD
- February 22 – National Wildlife Day #NationalWildlifeDay
- February 25 – Digital Learning Day #DLDay

Calender

Monday	Tuesday	Wednesday	Thursday	Friday	Saturday	Sunday
1	2	3	4	5	6	7
8	9	10	11	12	13	14
15	16	17	18	19	20	21
22	23	24	25	26	27	28
1	2	3	4	5	6	7

Notes

www.theezeragency.com

Content Strategy

Facebook
Account Name
Post Frequency
Content Ideas

Goals

Twitter
Account Name
Post Frequency
Content Ideas

Goals

Instagram
Account Name
Post Frequency
Content Ideas

Goals

Pinterest
Account Name
Post Frequency
Content Ideas

Goals

Media	No. of Subscribers	No. of Sales
Facebook		
Twitter		
Pinterest		
Instagram		

Blog Status

Notes

Monthly Paid Media Budget

Platform	Objective	Approved Budget
Total		

Audience Details

Platform:

Total expenses

Notes

Blog Post Monthly

Post title _____ Month of _____

Day	Title	Category	Done

Notes

The Blog Post

PUBLISH DATE	CATEGORY	POST TYPE
POST TITLE		
RELATED SERIES		

BLOG NOTES

DESCRIPTION
- ....
- ....
- ....
- ....
- ....

KEY POINTS
- ....
- ....
- ....
- ....
- ....

INPUT LINKS
- ....
- ....
- ....

SOCIAL MEDIA
☐ f ☐ 📷 ☐ p

OUTPUT LINKS
- ....
- ....
- ....

SPONSORS

GIVEAWAYS

FREEBIES

NOTES

The Blog Post

PUBLISH DATE	CATEGORY	POST TYPE

POST TITLE

RELATED SERIES

BLOG NOTES

DESCRIPTION

KEY POINTS

INPUT LINKS

SOCIAL MEDIA

f ◯ p

SPONSORS

GIVEAWAYS

FREEBIES

OUTPUT LINKS

NOTES

The Blog Post

PUBLISH DATE	CATEGORY	POST TYPE

POST TITLE

RELATED SERIES

Blog Notes

Description

Key Points

Input Links

Social Media

- f
-
-
- p

Output Links

SPONSORS

GIVEAWAYS

FREEBIES

Notes

The Blog Post

PUBLISH DATE	CATEGORY	POST TYPE
POST TITLE		
RELATED SERIES		

Blog Notes

Description

- ....
- ....
- ....
- ....
- ....

Key Points

- ....
- ....
- ....
- ....
- ....

Input Links

- ....
- ....
- ....

Social Media

☐ f ☐ ⓘ ☐ ☐ p

Output Links

- ....
- ....
- ....

SPONSORS

GIVEAWAYS

FREEBIES

Notes

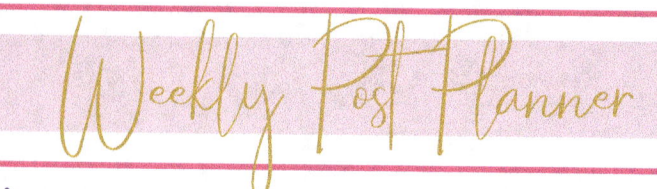

Weekly Post Planner

WEEK OF:

- DATE:
- BLOG TITLE:
- IDEAS:
- TAGS:
- CATEGORIES:
- KEYWORD PHRASE:
- CALL TO ACTION:
- AFFILIATE LINK TO PROMOTE:

TO DO:

POST PROMOTION:

WEEK OF:

- DATE:
- BLOG TITLE:
- IDEAS:
- TAGS:
- CATEGORIES:
- KEYWORD PHRASE:
- CALL TO ACTION:
- AFFILIATE LINK TO PROMOTE:

TO DO:

POST PROMOTION:

WEEK OF:

- DATE:
- BLOG TITLE:
- IDEAS:
- TAGS:
- CATEGORIES:
- KEYWORD PHRASE:
- CALL TO ACTION:
- AFFILIATE LINK TO PROMOTE:

TO DO:

POST PROMOTION:

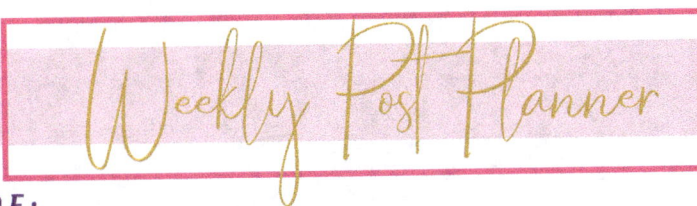

WEEK OF:

- DATE:
- BLOG TITLE:
- IDEAS:
- TAGS:
- CATEGORIES:
- KEYWORD PHRASE:
- CALL TO ACTION:
- AFFILIATE LINK TO PROMOTE:

TO DO:

POST PROMOTION:

WEEK OF:

- DATE:
- BLOG TITLE:
- IDEAS:
- TAGS:
- CATEGORIES:
- KEYWORD PHRASE:
- CALL TO ACTION:
- AFFILIATE LINK TO PROMOTE:

TO DO:

POST PROMOTION:

WEEK OF:

- DATE:
- BLOG TITLE:
- IDEAS:
- TAGS:
- CATEGORIES:
- KEYWORD PHRASE:
- CALL TO ACTION:
- AFFILIATE LINK TO PROMOTE:

TO DO:

POST PROMOTION:

Analytics

Total Users: [ ] New Users: [ ]

Page Views [ ] Bounce Rate [ ]

1 2 3 4 5 6 7 8 9 10 11 12

Pinterest Followers [ ] Pinterest Monthly Views [ ]

Email Subscribers [ ] New Subscribers [ ]

Instagram Followers [ ] Twitter Followers [ ]

Facebook Page Likes [ ] Facebook Group Members [ ]

Notes:

Community Management

Tasks

	M	T	W	T	F	S
	☐	☐	☐	☐	☐	☐
	☐	☐	☐	☐	☐	☐
	☐	☐	☐	☐	☐	☐
	☐	☐	☐	☐	☐	☐
	☐	☐	☐	☐	☐	☐
	☐	☐	☐	☐	☐	☐
	☐	☐	☐	☐	☐	☐
	☐	☐	☐	☐	☐	☐
	☐	☐	☐	☐	☐	☐
	☐	☐	☐	☐	☐	☐
	☐	☐	☐	☐	☐	☐
	☐	☐	☐	☐	☐	☐

Notes

March
Year 2021

"It is within everyone's grasp to be a CEO."
— Martha stewart

Monthly And Daily Socially Relevant Holidays

Theme for the month of March:

- American Red Cross Month
- National Women's History Month
- Social Work Month / Spiritual Wellness Month
- Women's History Month

March 2021 hashtag calendar:

- March 1 – National Peanut Butter Lover's Day #PeanutButterLoversDay
- March 2 – National Read Across America Day #ReadAcrossAmerica
- March 3 – World Wildlife Day #WorldWildlifeDay
- March 4 – National Grammar Day #GrammarDay
- March 4 – World Maths Day #MathsDay
- March 4 – National Pancake Day #NationalPancakeDay
- March 4 – World Book Day #WorldBookDay
- March 5 – National Day of Unplugging #DayOfUnplugging
- March 6 – National Employee Appreciation Day #EmployeeAppreciationDay
- March 6 – National Dentist's Day #DentistsDay
- March 7 – National Cereal Day #NationalCerealDay
- March 8 – International Women's Day #InternationalWomensDay #IWD2021 #EachforEqual
- March 8 – National Proofreading Day #NationalProofreadingDay
- March 9 – Organize Your Home Office Day #OrganizeYourHomeOfficeDay

Monthly And Daily Socially Relevant Holidays

March 2021 hashtag calendar:

- March 10 – Women & Girls HIV/AIDS Awareness Day #NWGHAAD
- March 12 – National Girl Scout Day #GirlScoutDay
- March 12 – Popcorn Lover's Day #PopcornLoversDay
- March 13 – World Sleep Day #WorldSleepDay
- March 14 – Potato Chip Day #NationalPotatoChipDay
- March 14 – Pi Day #PiDay
- March 14 – Daylight Savings #DaylightSavings
- March 15 – National Napping Day #NationalNappingDay
- March 16 – National Freedom of Information Day #FreedomOfInformationDay
- March 17 – St. Patrick's Day #StPatricksDay
- March 18 – Awkward Moments Day #NationalAwkwardMomentsDay
- March 19 – National Let's Laugh Day #NationalLetsLaughDay
- March 20 – First Day of Spring #FirstDayofSpring
- March 20 – International Day of Happiness #InternationalDayofHappiness
- March 20 – World Storytelling Day #WorldStorytellingDay
- March 21 – Elimination of Racial Discrimination Day #RacialDiscriminationDay
- March 21 – World Poetry Day #WorldPoetryDay
- March 22 – World Water Day #WorldWaterDay #Water2me
- March 23 – National Puppy Day #NationalPuppyDay
- March 25 – Tolkien Reading Day #TolkienReadingDay
- March 26 – National Spinach Day #NationalSpinachDay
- March 26 – Purple Day #PurpleDay
- March 27 – Earth Hour Day #EarthHourDay
- March 31 – Transgender Day of Visibility #TDOV

Calender

Monday	Tuesday	Wednesday	Thursday	Friday	Saturday	Sunday
1	2	3	4	5	6	7
8	9	10	11	12	13	14
15	16	17	18	19	20	21
22	23	24	25	26	27	28
29	30	31	1	2	3	4

Notes

www.theezeragency.com

Content Strategy

Facebook
Account Name
Post Frequency
Content Ideas

Goals

Twitter
Account Name
Post Frequency
Content Ideas

Goals

Instagram
Account Name
Post Frequency
Content Ideas

Goals

Pinterest
Account Name
Post Frequency
Content Ideas

Goals

Media	No. of Subscribers	No. of Sales
Facebook		
Twitter		
Pinterest		
Instagram		

Blog Status

Notes

Monthly Paid Media Budget

Platform	Objective	Approved Budget
Total		

Audience Details

Platform:

Total expenses

Notes

Post title _____ **Month of** _____

Day	Title	Category	Done

Notes

The Blog Post

PUBLISH DATE	CATEGORY	POST TYPE
POST TITLE		
RELATED SERIES		

BLOG NOTES

DESCRIPTION

- [ ] ....
- [ ] ....
- [ ] ....
- [ ] ....
- [ ] ....

KEY POINTS

- [ ] ....
- [ ] ....
- [ ] ....
- [ ] ....
- [ ] ....

INPUT LINKS

- [ ] ....
- [ ] ....
- [ ] ....

SOCIAL MEDIA

- [ ] f
- [ ] ⓘ
- [ ] p

OUTPUT LINKS

- [ ] ....
- [ ] ....
- [ ] ....

SPONSORS

GIVEAWAYS

FREEBIES

NOTES

PUBLISH DATE	CATEGORY	POST TYPE
POST TITLE		
RELATED SERIES		

BLOG NOTES

DESCRIPTION

- ....
- ....
- ....
- ....
- ....

KEY POINTS

- ....
- ....
- ....
- ....
- ....

INPUT LINKS

- ....
- ....
- ....

SOCIAL MEDIA

☐ f ☐ 📷 ☐ ☐ P

OUTPUT LINKS

- ....
- ....
- ....

SPONSORS

GIVEAWAYS

FREEBIES

NOTES

The Blog Post

PUBLISH DATE	CATEGORY	POST TYPE
POST TITLE		
RELATED SERIES		

Blog Notes

Description

-
-
-
-
-

Key Points

-
-
-
-
-

Input Links

-
-
-

Social Media

☐ f ☐ ⓘ ☐ ℗

Output Links

-
-
-

SPONSORS

GIVEAWAYS

FREEBIES

Notes

The Blog Post

PUBLISH DATE	CATEGORY	POST TYPE
POST TITLE		
RELATED SERIES		

BLOG NOTES

DESCRIPTION

- ....
- ....
- ....
- ....
- ....

KEY POINTS

- ....
- ....
- ....
- ....
- ....

INPUT LINKS

- ....
- ....
- ....

SOCIAL MEDIA

☐ f   ☐ ⓘ   ☐   ☐ P

OUTPUT LINKS

- ....
- ....
- ....

SPONSORS

GIVEAWAYS

FREEBIES

NOTES

Weekly Post Planner

WEEK OF:

- DATE:
- BLOG TITLE:
- IDEAS:
- TAGS:
- CATEGORIES:
- KEYWORD PHRASE:
- CALL TO ACTION:
- AFFILIATE LINK TO PROMOTE:

TO DO:

POST PROMOTION:

WEEK OF:

- DATE:
- BLOG TITLE:
- IDEAS:
- TAGS:
- CATEGORIES:
- KEYWORD PHRASE:
- CALL TO ACTION:
- AFFILIATE LINK TO PROMOTE:

TO DO:

POST PROMOTION:

WEEK OF:

- DATE:
- BLOG TITLE:
- IDEAS:
- TAGS:
- CATEGORIES:
- KEYWORD PHRASE:
- CALL TO ACTION:
- AFFILIATE LINK TO PROMOTE:

TO DO:

POST PROMOTION:

Weekly Post Planner

WEEK OF:

DATE:	
BLOG TITLE:	
IDEAS:	
TAGS:	
CATEGORIES:	
KEYWORD PHRASE:	
CALL TO ACTION:	
AFFILIATE LINK TO PROMOTE:	

TO DO:

POST PROMOTION:

WEEK OF:

DATE:	
BLOG TITLE:	
IDEAS:	
TAGS:	
CATEGORIES:	
KEYWORD PHRASE:	
CALL TO ACTION:	
AFFILIATE LINK TO PROMOTE:	

TO DO:

POST PROMOTION:

WEEK OF:

DATE:	
BLOG TITLE:	
IDEAS:	
TAGS:	
CATEGORIES:	
KEYWORD PHRASE:	
CALL TO ACTION:	
AFFILIATE LINK TO PROMOTE:	

TO DO:

POST PROMOTION:

Analytics

Total Users: [ ] New Users: [ ]

Page Views: [ ] Bounce Rate: [ ]

| 1 | 2 | 3 | 4 | 5 | 6 | 7 | 8 | 9 | 10 | 11 | 12 |

Pinterest Followers: [ ] Pinterest Monthly Views: [ ]

Email Subscribers: [ ] New Subscribers: [ ]

Instagram Followers: [ ] Twitter Followers: [ ]

Facebook Page Likes: [ ] Facebook Group Members: [ ]

Notes:

Community Management

Tasks

	M	T	W	T	F	S
	☐	☐	☐	☐	☐	☐
	☐	☐	☐	☐	☐	☐
	☐	☐	☐	☐	☐	☐
	☐	☐	☐	☐	☐	☐
	☐	☐	☐	☐	☐	☐
	☐	☐	☐	☐	☐	☐
	☐	☐	☐	☐	☐	☐
	☐	☐	☐	☐	☐	☐
	☐	☐	☐	☐	☐	☐
	☐	☐	☐	☐	☐	☐
	☐	☐	☐	☐	☐	☐
	☐	☐	☐	☐	☐	☐

Notes

April
Year 2021

> "We need to get women to the point where they aren't apologizing. It's time to take ownership in our success."
> – Tory Burch

Monthly And Daily Socially Relevant Holidays

Themes for the month of April:

- Celebrate Diversity Month
- National Poetry Month
- Stress Awareness Month

Weeks of observance in April:

- Ramadan: April 12 – May 11

April 2021 hashtag calendar:

- April 1 – April Fools Day #AprilFools
- April 1 – National Walking Day #NationalWalkingDay
- April 2 – World Autism Awareness Day #WAAD
- April 3 – Find a Rainbow Day #FindARainbowDay
- April 4 – Hug a Newsperson Day #HugANewsperson
- April 7 – World Health Day #LetsTalk
- April 10 – National Siblings Day #NationalSiblingsDay
- April 10 – Encourage a Young Writer Day #EncourageAYoungWriterDay
- April 11 – National Pet Day #NationalPetDay
- April 12 – International Day of Human Space Flight #HumanSpaceFlightDay
- April 15 – Academy Awards #AcademyAwards
- April 15 – National Tax Day #TaxDay

Monthly And Daily Socially Relevant Holidays

April 2021 hashtag calendar:

- April 15 – Get to Know Your Customers Day #GetToKnowYourCustomersDay
- April 15 – National High-Five Day #NH5D
- April 16 – National Stress Awareness Day #StressAwarenessDay
- April 16 – Wear Your Pajamas to Work Day #PJDay
- April 17 – Haiku Poetry Day #HaikuPoetryDay
- April 20 – National Look-Alike Day #NationalLookAlikeDay
- April 21 – National Administrative Professionals Day #AdministrativeProfessionalsDay
- April 22 – Earth Day #EarthDay2021
- April 22 – Take Our Daughters & Sons to Work Day #COUNTONME
- April 23 – National Picnic Day #NationalPicnicDay
- April 25 – World Malaria Day #EndMalariaForGood
- April 28 – Denim Day #DenimDay
- April 29 – International Dance Day #InternationalDanceDay
- April 30 – National Honesty Day #NationalHonestyDay
- April 30 – International Jazz Day #JazzDay
- April 30 – National Adopt a Shelter Pet Day #AdoptAShelterPetDay
- April 30 – Arbor Day #ArborDay

Calender

Monday	Tuesday	Wednesday	Thursday	Friday	Saturday	Sunday
29	30	31	1	2	3	4
5	6	7	8	9	10	11
12	13	14	15	16	17	18
19	20	21	22	23	24	25
26	27	28	29	30	1	2

Notes

www.theezeragency.com

Content Strategy

Facebook
Account Name
Post Frequency
Content Ideas

Goals

Twitter
Account Name
Post Frequency
Content Ideas

Goals

Instagram
Account Name
Post Frequency
Content Ideas

Goals

Pinterest
Account Name
Post Frequency
Content Ideas

Goals

Media	No. of Subscribers	No. of Sales
Facebook		
Twitter		
Pinterest		
Instagram		

Blog Status

Notes

Monthly Paid Media Budget

Platform	Objective	Approved Budget
Total		

Audience Details

Platform:

Total expenses

Notes

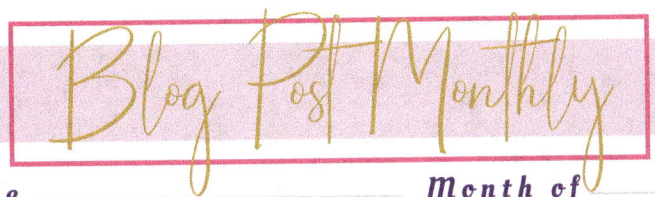

Post title _____ *Month of* _____

Day	Title	Category	Done

Notes

The Blog Post

PUBLISH DATE	CATEGORY	POST TYPE
POST TITLE		
RELATED SERIES		

BLOG NOTES

DESCRIPTION

-
-
-
-
-

KEY POINTS

-
-
-
-
-

INPUT LINKS

-
-
-

SOCIAL MEDIA

- f
-
- p

OUTPUT LINKS

-
-
-

SPONSORS

GIVEAWAYS

FREEBIES

NOTES

The Blog Post

PUBLISH DATE	CATEGORY	POST TYPE

POST TITLE

RELATED SERIES

BLOG NOTES

DESCRIPTION
-
-
-
-
-

KEY POINTS
-
-
-
-
-

INPUT LINKS
-
-
-

SOCIAL MEDIA
☐ f ☐ 📷 ☐ ☐ p

OUTPUT LINKS
-
-
-

SPONSORS

GIVEAWAYS

FREEBIES

NOTES

The Blog Post

| PUBLISH DATE | CATEGORY | POST TYPE |

POST TITLE

RELATED SERIES

BLOG NOTES

DESCRIPTION

KEY POINTS

INPUT LINKS

SOCIAL MEDIA

f   instagram   p

OUTPUT LINKS

SPONSORS

GIVEAWAYS

FREEBIES

NOTES

The Blog Post

PUBLISH DATE	CATEGORY	POST TYPE
POST TITLE		
RELATED SERIES		

BLOG NOTES

DESCRIPTION

- ....
- ....
- ....
- ....
- ....

KEY POINTS

- ....
- ....
- ....
- ....
- ....

INPUT LINKS

- ....
- ....
- ....

SOCIAL MEDIA

☐ f   ☐ ⓘ   ☐   ☐ ℗

SPONSORS

GIVEAWAYS

FREEBIES

OUTPUT LINKS

- ....
- ....
- ....

NOTES

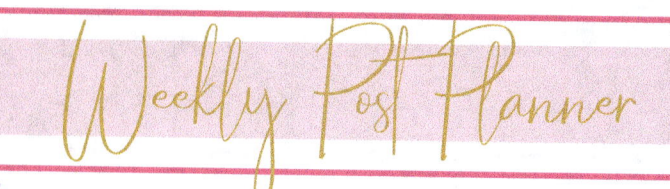

Weekly Post Planner

WEEK OF:

DATE:
BLOG TITLE:
IDEAS:

TAGS:
CATEGORIES:
KEYWORD PHRASE:
CALL TO ACTION:
AFFILIATE LINK TO PROMOTE:

TO DO:

POST PROMOTION:

WEEK OF:

DATE:
BLOG TITLE:
IDEAS:

TAGS:
CATEGORIES:
KEYWORD PHRASE:
CALL TO ACTION:
AFFILIATE LINK TO PROMOTE:

TO DO:

POST PROMOTION:

WEEK OF:

DATE:
BLOG TITLE:
IDEAS:

TAGS:
CATEGORIES:
KEYWORD PHRASE:
CALL TO ACTION:
AFFILIATE LINK TO PROMOTE:

TO DO:

POST PROMOTION:

WEEK OF:

- DATE:
- BLOG TITLE:
- IDEAS:

- TAGS:
- CATEGORIES:
- KEYWORD PHRASE:
- CALL TO ACTION:
- AFFILIATE LINK TO PROMOTE:

TO DO:

POST PROMOTION:

WEEK OF:

- DATE:
- BLOG TITLE:
- IDEAS:

- TAGS:
- CATEGORIES:
- KEYWORD PHRASE:
- CALL TO ACTION:
- AFFILIATE LINK TO PROMOTE:

TO DO:

POST PROMOTION:

WEEK OF:

- DATE:
- BLOG TITLE:
- IDEAS:

- TAGS:
- CATEGORIES:
- KEYWORD PHRASE:
- CALL TO ACTION:
- AFFILIATE LINK TO PROMOTE:

TO DO:

POST PROMOTION:

Analytics

Total Users: New Users:

Page Views Bounce Rate

| 1 | 2 | 3 | 4 | 5 | 6 | 7 | 8 | 9 | 10 | 11 | 12 |

Pinterest Followers Pinterest Monthly Views

Email Subscribers New Subscribers

Instagram Followers Twitter Followers

Facebook Page Likes Facebook Group Members

Notes:

Community Management

Tasks

	M	T	W	T	F	S
	☐	☐	☐	☐	☐	☐
	☐	☐	☐	☐	☐	☐
	☐	☐	☐	☐	☐	☐
	☐	☐	☐	☐	☐	☐
	☐	☐	☐	☐	☐	☐
	☐	☐	☐	☐	☐	☐
	☐	☐	☐	☐	☐	☐
	☐	☐	☐	☐	☐	☐
	☐	☐	☐	☐	☐	☐
	☐	☐	☐	☐	☐	☐
	☐	☐	☐	☐	☐	☐
	☐	☐	☐	☐	☐	☐

Notes

May
Year 2021

"You will be defined not just by what you achieve, but y how you survive."
— Sheryl sanderg

Monthly And Daily Socially Relevant Holidays

Themes for the month of May:

- Asian American Month
- Lupus Awareness Month
- Family Wellness Month
- National Barbecue Month

Weeks of observance in May:

- Ramadan: April 12 – May 11

Monthly And Daily Socially Relevant Holidays

May 2021 hashtag calendar:

- May 1 – International Workers Day #IntWorkersDay
- May 1 – May Day #MayDay
- May 3 – World Press Freedom Day #WPFD2020
- May 4 – Star Wars Day #StarWarsDay
- May 4 – International Firefighters Day #InternationalFirefightersDay
- May 4 – Thank a Teacher Day #ThankATeacher
- May 5 – Cinco de Mayo #CincoDeMayo
- May 5 – World Asthma Day #WorldAsthmaDay
- May 6 – National Nurses Day #NursesDay
- May 7 – World Password Day #WorldPasswordDay
- May 9 – Europe Day #EuropeDay
- May 9 – Mother's Day #MothersDay
- May 10 – World Lupus Day #LupusDay
- May 12 – National Limerick Day #NationalLimerickDay
- May 12 – National Receptionist Day #NationalReceptionistDay
- May 15 – International Day of Families #FamilyDay
- May 15 – National Chocolate Chip Day #ChocolateChipDay
- May 16 – Love a Tree Day #LoveATreeDay
- May 17 – Day Against Homophobia & Transphobia #IDAHOT
- May 21 – Endangered Species Day #EndangeredSpeciesDay
- May 24 – National Scavenger Hunt Day #NationalScavengerHuntDay
- May 28 – Hamburger Day #NationalHamburgerDay
- May 28 – Heat Awareness Day #NoFryDay
- May 30 – National Creativity Day #NationalCreativityDay
- May 31 – World No-Tobacco Day #NoTobacco
- May 31 – Memorial Day #MemorialDay

Calender

Monday	Tuesday	Wednesday	Thursday	Friday	Saturday	Sunday
26	27	28	29	30	1	2
3	4	5	6	7	8	9
10	11	12	13	14	15	16
17	18	19	20	21	22	23
24	25	26	27	28	29	30
31	1	2	3	4	5	6

Notes

Content Strategy

Facebook
Account Name
Post Frequency
Content Ideas

Goals

Twitter
Account Name
Post Frequency
Content Ideas

Goals

Instagram
Account Name
Post Frequency
Content Ideas

Goals

Pinterest
Account Name
Post Frequency
Content Ideas

Goals

Media	No. of Subscribers	No. of Sales
Facebook		
Twitter		
Pinterest		
Instagram		

Blog Status

Notes

Monthly Paid Media Budget

Platform	Objective	Approved Budget
Total		

Audience Details

Platform:

Total expenses

Notes

Blog Post Monthly

Post title _____   **Month of** _____

Day	Title	Category	Done

Notes

The Blog Post

PUBLISH DATE	CATEGORY	POST TYPE
POST TITLE		
RELATED SERIES		

BLOG NOTES

DESCRIPTION

-
-
-
-
-

KEY POINTS

-
-
-
-
-

INPUT LINKS

-
-
-

SOCIAL MEDIA

☐ f   ☐ ⌾   ☐ ℗

OUTPUT LINKS

-
-
-

SPONSORS

GIVEAWAYS

FREEBIES

NOTES

The Blog Post

| PUBLISH DATE | CATEGORY | POST TYPE |

POST TITLE

RELATED SERIES

BLOG NOTES

DESCRIPTION

KEY POINTS

INPUT LINKS

SOCIAL MEDIA

f ◯ p

OUTPUT LINKS

SPONSORS

GIVEAWAYS

FREEBIES

NOTES

The Blog Post

PUBLISH DATE	CATEGORY	POST TYPE
POST TITLE		
RELATED SERIES		

BLOG NOTES

DESCRIPTION

KEY POINTS

INPUT LINKS

SOCIAL MEDIA

☐ f   ☐ 📷   ☐ p

OUTPUT LINKS

SPONSORS

GIVEAWAYS

FREEBIES

NOTES

The Blog Post

PUBLISH DATE	CATEGORY	POST TYPE
POST TITLE		
RELATED SERIES		

DESCRIPTION

DESCRIPTION

KEY POINTS

INPUT LINKS

SOCIAL MEDIA

☐ f ☐ ⧇ ☐ ☐ ℘

OUTPUT LINKS

SPONSORS

GIVEAWAYS

FREEBIES

NOTES

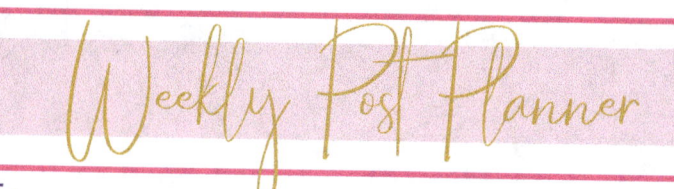

Weekly Post Planner

WEEK OF:

- DATE:
- BLOG TITLE:
- IDEAS:
- TAGS:
- CATEGORIES:
- KEYWORD PHRASE:
- CALL TO ACTION:
- AFFILIATE LINK TO PROMOTE:

TO DO:

POST PROMOTION:

WEEK OF:

- DATE:
- BLOG TITLE:
- IDEAS:
- TAGS:
- CATEGORIES:
- KEYWORD PHRASE:
- CALL TO ACTION:
- AFFILIATE LINK TO PROMOTE:

TO DO:

POST PROMOTION:

WEEK OF:

- DATE:
- BLOG TITLE:
- IDEAS:
- TAGS:
- CATEGORIES:
- KEYWORD PHRASE:
- CALL TO ACTION:

TO DO:

POST PROMOTION:

WEEK OF:

DATE:
BLOG TITLE:
IDEAS:

TAGS:
CATEGORIES:
KEYWORD PHRASE:
CALL TO ACTION:
AFFILIATE LINK TO PROMOTE:

TO DO:

POST PROMOTION:

WEEK OF:

DATE:
BLOG TITLE:
IDEAS:

TAGS:
CATEGORIES:
KEYWORD PHRASE:
CALL TO ACTION:
AFFILIATE LINK TO PROMOTE:

TO DO:

POST PROMOTION:

WEEK OF:

DATE:
BLOG TITLE:
IDEAS:

TAGS:
CATEGORIES:
KEYWORD PHRASE:
CALL TO ACTION:

TO DO:

POST PROMOTION:

Analytics

Total Users: New Users:

Page Views Bounce Rate

| 1 | 2 | 3 | 4 | 5 | 6 | 7 | 8 | 9 | 10 | 11 | 12 |

Pinterest Followers Pinterest Monthly Views

Email Subscribers New Subscribers

Instagram Followers Twitter Followers

Facebook Page Likes Facebook Group Members

Notes:

Community Management

Tasks

	M	T	W	T	F	S
	☐	☐	☐	☐	☐	☐
	☐	☐	☐	☐	☐	☐
	☐	☐	☐	☐	☐	☐
	☐	☐	☐	☐	☐	☐
	☐	☐	☐	☐	☐	☐
	☐	☐	☐	☐	☐	☐
	☐	☐	☐	☐	☐	☐
	☐	☐	☐	☐	☐	☐
	☐	☐	☐	☐	☐	☐
	☐	☐	☐	☐	☐	☐
	☐	☐	☐	☐	☐	☐
	☐	☐	☐	☐	☐	☐

Notes

June
Year 2021

"Don't give up on something just because you think you can't do it."
-Chanda Kochhar

Monthly And Daily Socially Relevant Holidays

Themes for the month of June:

- LGBTQ Pride Month
- Men's Health Education and Awareness Month

June 2021 hashtag calendar:

- June 4 – National Donut Day #NationalDonutDay
- June 5 – World Environment Day #WorldEnvironmentDay
- June 6 – Higher Education Day #HigherEducationDay
- June 6 – National Cancer Survivor's Day #NCSD2021
- June 8 – World Oceans Day #WorldOceansDay
- June 8 – Best Friends Day #BestFriendsDay
- June 11 – Make Life Beautiful Day #MakeLifeBeautiful
- June 14 – National Flag Day #FlagDay
- June 14 – World Blood Donor Day #GiveBlood
- June 20 – World Refugee Day #WorldRefugeeDay
- June 20 – First Day of Summer #FirstDayOfSummer
- June 20 – Father's Day #FathersDay
- June 21 – National Selfie Day #NationalSelfieDay
- June 21 – World Music Day #WorldMusicDay
- June 21 – International Yoga Day #InternationalYogaDay
- June 23 – National Columnists' Day #NationalColumnistDay
- June 27 – National Sunglasses Day #NationalSunglassesDay
- June 30 – Social Media Day #SMDay, #SocialMediaDay

Calender

Monday	Tuesday	Wednesday	Thursday	Friday	Saturday	Sunday
31	1	2	3	4	5	6
7	8	9	10	11	12	13
14	15	16	17	18	19	20
21	22	23	24	25	26	27
28	29	30	1	2	3	4

Notes

www.theezeragency.com

Content Strategy

Facebook
Account Name
Post Frequency
Content Ideas

Goals

Twitter
Account Name
Post Frequency
Content Ideas

Goals

Instagram
Account Name
Post Frequency
Content Ideas

Goals

Pinterest
Account Name
Post Frequency
Content Ideas

Goals

Media	No. of Subscribers	No. of Sales
Facebook		
Twitter		
Pinterest		
Instagram		

Blog Status

Notes

Monthly Paid Media Budget

Platform	Objective	Approved Budget

Total

Audience Details

Platform:

Total expenses

Notes

Post title _____   Month of _____

Day	Title	Category	Done

Notes

The Blog Post

| PUBLISH DATE | CATEGORY | POST TYPE |

POST TITLE

RELATED SERIES

BLOG NOTES

DESCRIPTION

- ....
- ....
- ....
- ....
- ....

KEY POINTS

- ....
- ....
- ....
- ....
- ....

INPUT LINKS

- ....
- ....
- ....

SOCIAL MEDIA

☐ f ☐ 📷 ☐   ☐ P

OUTPUT LINKS

- ....
- ....
- ....

SPONSORS

GIVEAWAYS

FREEBIES

NOTES

The Blog Post

PUBLISH DATE	CATEGORY	POST TYPE
POST TITLE		
RELATED SERIES		

Blog Notes

Description

-
-
-
-
-

Key Points

-
-
-
-
-

Input Links

-
-
-

Social Media

- [ ] Facebook
- [ ] Instagram
- [ ] Pinterest

Output Links

-
-
-

SPONSORS

GIVEAWAYS

FREEBIES

Notes

PUBLISH DATE	CATEGORY	POST TYPE
POST TITLE		
RELATED SERIES		

BLOG NOTES

DESCRIPTION

-
-
-
-
-

KEY POINTS

-
-
-
-
-

INPUT LINKS

-
-
-

SOCIAL MEDIA

☐ f ☐ ⊙ ☐ p

OUTPUT LINKS

-
-
-

SPONSORS

GIVEAWAYS

FREEBIES

NOTES

The Blog Post

PUBLISH DATE	CATEGORY	POST TYPE
POST TITLE		
RELATED SERIES		

BLOG NOTES

DESCRIPTION
- ....
- ....
- ....
- ....
- ....

KEY POINTS
- ....
- ....
- ....
- ....
- ....

INPUT LINKS
- ....
- ....
- ....

SOCIAL MEDIA
☐ f   ☐ ◉   ☐ ᵖ

OUTPUT LINKS
- ....
- ....
- ....

SPONSORS

GIVEAWAYS

FREEBIES

NOTES

Weekly Post Planner

WEEK OF:

- DATE:
- BLOG TITLE:
- IDEAS:
- TAGS:
- CATEGORIES:
- KEYWORD PHRASE:
- CALL TO ACTION:
- AFFILIATE LINK TO PROMOTE:

TO DO:

POST PROMOTION:

WEEK OF:

- DATE:
- BLOG TITLE:
- IDEAS:
- TAGS:
- CATEGORIES:
- KEYWORD PHRASE:
- CALL TO ACTION:
- AFFILIATE LINK TO PROMOTE:

TO DO:

POST PROMOTION:

WEEK OF:

- DATE:
- BLOG TITLE:
- IDEAS:
- TAGS:
- CATEGORIES:
- KEYWORD PHRASE:
- CALL TO ACTION:
- AFFILIATE LINK TO PROMOTE:

TO DO:

POST PROMOTION:

Weekly Post Planner

WEEK OF:

- DATE:
- BLOG TITLE:
- IDEAS:
- TAGS:
- CATEGORIES:
- KEYWORD PHRASE:
- CALL TO ACTION:
- AFFILIATE LINK TO PROMOTE:

TO DO:

POST PROMOTION:

WEEK OF:

- DATE:
- BLOG TITLE:
- IDEAS:
- TAGS:
- CATEGORIES:
- KEYWORD PHRASE:
- CALL TO ACTION:
- AFFILIATE LINK TO PROMOTE:

TO DO:

POST PROMOTION:

WEEK OF:

- DATE:
- BLOG TITLE:
- IDEAS:
- TAGS:
- CATEGORIES:
- KEYWORD PHRASE:
- CALL TO ACTION:
- AFFILIATE LINK TO PROMOTE:

TO DO:

POST PROMOTION:

Analytics

Total Users: ☐   New Users: ☐

Page Views ☐   Bounce Rate ☐

1	2	3	4	5	6	7	8	9	10	11	12

Pinterest Followers ☐   Pinterest Monthly Views ☐

Email Subscribers ☐   New Subscribers ☐

Instagram Followers ☐   Twitter Followers ☐

Facebook Page Likes ☐   Facebook Group Members ☐

Notes:

Community Management

Tasks

	M	T	W	T	F	S
	☐	☐	☐	☐	☐	☐
	☐	☐	☐	☐	☐	☐
	☐	☐	☐	☐	☐	☐
	☐	☐	☐	☐	☐	☐
	☐	☐	☐	☐	☐	☐
	☐	☐	☐	☐	☐	☐
	☐	☐	☐	☐	☐	☐
	☐	☐	☐	☐	☐	☐
	☐	☐	☐	☐	☐	☐
	☐	☐	☐	☐	☐	☐
	☐	☐	☐	☐	☐	☐
	☐	☐	☐	☐	☐	☐

Notes

July
Year 2021

"Always stay true to yourself and never let what somebody says distract you from your goals."
-Michelle Obama

Monthly And Daily Socially Relevant Holidays

Themes for the month of July:

National Grilling Month
National Ice Cream Month

July 2021 hashtag calendar:

July 1 – National Postal Worker Day #NationalPostalWorkerDay
July 2 – World UFO Day #WorldUFODay
July 4 – Independence Day #July4th
July 7 – World Chocolate Day #WorldChocolateDay
July 11 – Cheer Up the Lonely Day #CheerUpTheLonelyDay
July 12 – Malala Day #MalalaDay
July 12 – National Simplicity Day – #NationalSimplicityDay
July 15 – Give Something Away Day #GiveSomethingAwayDay
July 15 – Get to Know Your Customers Day #GetToKnowYourCustomersDay
July 17 – World Emoji Day #WorldEmojiDay
July 18 – Nelson Mandela International Day #MandelaDay
July 30 – International Day of Friendship #DayOfFriendship

Calender

Monday	Tuesday	Wednesday	Thursday	Friday	Saturday	Sunday
28	29	30	1	2	3	4
5	6	7	8	9	10	11
12	13	14	15	16	17	18
19	20	21	22	23	24	25
26	27	28	29	30	31	1

Notes

www.theezeragency.com

Content Strategy

Facebook
Account Name
Post Frequency
Content Ideas

Goals

Twitter
Account Name
Post Frequency
Content Ideas

Goals

Instagram
Account Name
Post Frequency
Content Ideas

Goals

Pinterest
Account Name
Post Frequency
Content Ideas

Goals

Media	No. of Subscribers	No. of Sales
Facebook		
Twitter		
Pinterest		
Instagram		

Blog Status

Notes

Monthly Paid Media Budget

Platform	Objective	Approved Budget
Total		

Audience Details

Platform:

Total expenses

Notes

Blog Post Monthly

Post title _____ Month of _____

Day	Title	Category	Done

Notes

PUBLISH DATE	CATEGORY	POST TYPE
POST TITLE		
RELATED SERIES		

BLOG NOTES

DESCRIPTION

- ....
- ....
- ....
- ....
- ....

KEY POINTS

- ....
- ....
- ....
- ....
- ....

INPUT LINKS

- ....
- ....
- ....

SOCIAL MEDIA

☐ f   ☐ 📷   ☐ p

OUTPUT LINKS

- ....
- ....
- ....

SPONSORS

GIVEAWAYS

FREEBIES

NOTES

The Blog Post

PUBLISH DATE	CATEGORY	POST TYPE
POST TITLE		
RELATED SERIES		

BLOG NOTES

DESCRIPTION

-
-
-
-
-

KEY POINTS

-
-
-
-
-

INPUT LINKS

-
-
-

SOCIAL MEDIA

☐ f ☐ ⓘ ☐ ☐ p

OUTPUT LINKS

-
-
-

SPONSORS

GIVEAWAYS

FREEBIES

NOTES

The Blog Post

PUBLISH DATE	CATEGORY	POST TYPE
POST TITLE		
RELATED SERIES		

BLOG NOTES

DESCRIPTION

- [ ]
- [ ]
- [ ]
- [ ]
- [ ]

KEY POINTS

- [ ]
- [ ]
- [ ]
- [ ]
- [ ]

INPUT LINKS

- [ ]
- [ ]
- [ ]

SOCIAL MEDIA

- [ ] f
- [ ] Instagram
- [ ] Pinterest

OUTPUT LINKS

- [ ]
- [ ]
- [ ]

SPONSORS

GIVEAWAYS

FREEBIES

NOTES

The Blog Post

PUBLISH DATE	CATEGORY	POST TYPE
POST TITLE		
RELATED SERIES		

Blog Notes

Description

-
-
-
-
-

Key Points

-
-
-
-
-

Input Links

-
-
-

Social Media

☐ f   ☐ 📷   ☐ p

Output Links

-
-
-

SPONSORS

GIVEAWAYS

FREEBIES

Notes

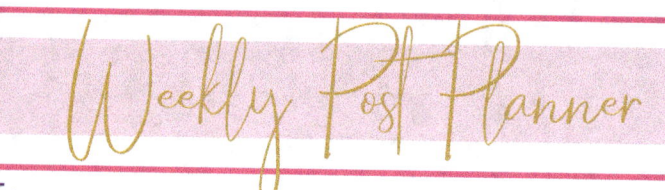

Weekly Post Planner

WEEK OF:

- DATE:
- BLOG TITLE:
- IDEAS:
- TAGS:
- CATEGORIES:
- KEYWORD PHRASE:
- CALL TO ACTION:
- AFFILIATE LINK TO PROMOTE:

TO DO:

POST PROMOTION:

WEEK OF:

- DATE:
- BLOG TITLE:
- IDEAS:
- TAGS:
- CATEGORIES:
- KEYWORD PHRASE:
- CALL TO ACTION:
- AFFILIATE LINK TO PROMOTE:

TO DO:

POST PROMOTION:

WEEK OF:

- DATE:
- BLOG TITLE:
- IDEAS:
- TAGS:
- CATEGORIES:
- KEYWORD PHRASE:
- CALL TO ACTION:
- AFFILIATE LINK TO PROMOTE:

TO DO:

POST PROMOTION:

Weekly Post Planner

WEEK OF:

- DATE:
- BLOG TITLE:
- IDEAS:
- TAGS:
- CATEGORIES:
- KEYWORD PHRASE:
- CALL TO ACTION:
- AFFILIATE LINK TO PROMOTE:

TO DO:

POST PROMOTION:

WEEK OF:

- DATE:
- BLOG TITLE:
- IDEAS:
- TAGS:
- CATEGORIES:
- KEYWORD PHRASE:
- CALL TO ACTION:
- AFFILIATE LINK TO PROMOTE:

TO DO:

POST PROMOTION:

WEEK OF:

- DATE:
- BLOG TITLE:
- IDEAS:
- TAGS:
- CATEGORIES:
- KEYWORD PHRASE:
- CALL TO ACTION:
- AFFILIATE LINK TO PROMOTE:

TO DO:

POST PROMOTION:

Analytics

Total Users: ☐   New Users: ☐

Page Views: ☐   Bounce Rate: ☐

| 1 | 2 | 3 | 4 | 5 | 6 | 7 | 8 | 9 | 10 | 11 | 12 |

Pinterest Followers: ☐   Pinterest Monthly Views: ☐

Email Subscribers: ☐   New Subscribers: ☐

Instagram Followers: ☐   Twitter Followers: ☐

Facebook Page Likes: ☐   Facebook Group Members: ☐

Notes:

Community Management

Tasks	M	T	W	T	F	S

Notes

August
Year 2021

"There is no force more powerful than a woman determined to rise"
-Dorothy Dandridge

Monthly And Daily Socially Relevant Holiday

Themes for the month of August:

- American Artists Appreciation Month
- Black Business Month
- National Immunization Awareness Month

August 2021 hashtag calendar:

- August 1 – Planner Day #PlannerDay
- August 1 – American Family Day #AmericanFamilyDay
- August 2 – National Coloring Book Day #NationalColoringBookDay
- August 8 – International Cat Day #InternationalCatDay
- August 9 – National Book Lovers Day #NationalBookLoversDay
- August 11 – National Sons and Daughters Day #SonsAndDaughtersDay
- August 12 – International Youth Day #YouthDay
- August 12 – World Elephant Day #WorldElephantDay
- August 13 – International Lefthanders Day #LefthandersDay
- August 15 – National Relaxation Day #NationalRelaxationDay
- August 16 – National Tell a Joke Day #NationalTellAJokeDay
- August 19 – World Photo Day #WorldPhotoDay
- August 19 – World Humanitarian Day #WorldHumanitarianDay
- August 20 – National Lemonade Day #NationalLemonadeDay
- August 26 – National Dog Day #NationalDogDay
- August 26 – National Women's Equality Day #WomensEqualityDay

Calender

Monday	Tuesday	Wednesday	Thursday	Friday	Saturday	Sunday
26	27	28	29	30	31	1
2	3	4	5	6	7	8
9	10	11	12	13	14	15
16	17	18	19	20	21	22
23/30	24/31	25	26	27	28	29

Notes

www.theezeragency.com

Content Strategy

Facebook
Account Name
Post Frequency
Content Ideas

Goals

Twitter
Account Name
Post Frequency
Content Ideas

Goals

Instagram
Account Name
Post Frequency
Content Ideas

Goals

Pinterest
Account Name
Post Frequency
Content Ideas

Goals

Media	No. of Subscribers	No. of Sales
Facebook		
Twitter		
Pinterest		
Instagram		

Blog Status

Notes

Monthly Paid Media Budget

Platform	Objective	Approved Budget

Total

Audience Details

Platform:

Notes

Total expenses

Post title _____ Month of _____

Day	Title	Category	Done

Notes

The Blog Post

| PUBLISH DATE | CATEGORY | POST TYPE |

POST TITLE

RELATED SERIES

BLOG NOTES

DESCRIPTION

KEY POINTS

INPUT LINKS

SOCIAL MEDIA

f ⬚ ⬚ p

OUTPUT LINKS

SPONSORS

GIVEAWAYS

FREEBIES

NOTES

The Blog Post

PUBLISH DATE	CATEGORY	POST TYPE
POST TITLE		
RELATED SERIES		

Blog Notes

Description
-
-
-
-
-

Key Points
-
-
-
-
-

Input Links
-
-
-

Social Media
☐ f   ☐ ⦿   ☐ p

Output Links
-
-
-

SPONSORS

GIVEAWAYS

FREEBIES

Notes

The Blog Post

PUBLISH DATE	CATEGORY	POST TYPE

POST TITLE

RELATED SERIES

BLOG NOTES

DESCRIPTION

KEY POINTS

INPUT LINKS

SOCIAL MEDIA
☐ f ☐ 📷 ☐ ☐ p

OUTPUT LINKS

SPONSORS

GIVEAWAYS

FREEBIES

NOTES

The Blog Post

PUBLISH DATE	CATEGORY	POST TYPE
POST TITLE		
RELATED SERIES		

BLOG NOTES

DESCRIPTION

- ☐ ....
- ☐ ....
- ☐ ....
- ☐ ....
- ☐ ....

KEY POINTS

- ☐ ....
- ☐ ....
- ☐ ....
- ☐ ....
- ☐ ....

INPUT LINKS

- ☐ ....
- ☐ ....
- ☐ ....

SOCIAL MEDIA

☐ f   ☐ 📷   ☐ P

OUTPUT LINKS

- ☐ ....
- ☐ ....
- ☐ ....

SPONSORS

GIVEAWAYS

FREEBIES

NOTES

Weekly Post Planner

WEEK OF:

DATE:
BLOG TITLE:
IDEAS:

TAGS:
CATEGORIES:
KEYWORD PHRASE:
CALL TO ACTION:
AFFILIATE LINK TO PROMOTE:

TO DO:

POST PROMOTION:
f ⊙ ℗

WEEK OF:

DATE:
BLOG TITLE:
IDEAS:

TAGS:
CATEGORIES:
KEYWORD PHRASE:
CALL TO ACTION:
AFFILIATE LINK TO PROMOTE:

TO DO:

POST PROMOTION:
f ⊙ ℗

WEEK OF:

DATE:
BLOG TITLE:
IDEAS:

TAGS:
CATEGORIES:
KEYWORD PHRASE:
CALL TO ACTION:
AFFILIATE LINK TO PROMOTE:

TO DO:

POST PROMOTION:
f ⊙ ℗

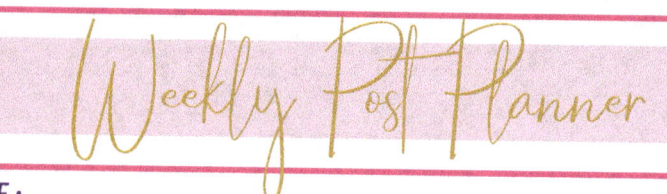

Weekly Post Planner

WEEK OF:

- DATE:
- BLOG TITLE:
- IDEAS:
- TAGS:
- CATEGORIES:
- KEYWORD PHRASE:
- CALL TO ACTION:
- AFFILIATE LINK TO PROMOTE:

TO DO:

POST PROMOTION:

WEEK OF:

- DATE:
- BLOG TITLE:
- IDEAS:
- TAGS:
- CATEGORIES:
- KEYWORD PHRASE:
- CALL TO ACTION:
- AFFILIATE LINK TO PROMOTE:

TO DO:

POST PROMOTION:

WEEK OF:

- DATE:
- BLOG TITLE:
- IDEAS:
- TAGS:
- CATEGORIES:
- KEYWORD PHRASE:
- CALL TO ACTION:
- AFFILIATE LINK TO PROMOTE:

TO DO:

POST PROMOTION:

Analytics

Total Users:

Page Views

New Users:

Bounce Rate

| 1 | 2 | 3 | 4 | 5 | 6 | 7 | 8 | 9 | 10 | 11 | 12 |

Pinterest Followers

Pinterest Monthly Views

Email Subscribers

New Subscribers

Instagram Followers

Twitter Followers

Facebook Page Likes

Facebook Group Members

Notes:

Community Management

Tasks

	M	T	W	T	F	S
	☐	☐	☐	☐	☐	☐
	☐	☐	☐	☐	☐	☐
	☐	☐	☐	☐	☐	☐
	☐	☐	☐	☐	☐	☐
	☐	☐	☐	☐	☐	☐
	☐	☐	☐	☐	☐	☐
	☐	☐	☐	☐	☐	☐
	☐	☐	☐	☐	☐	☐
	☐	☐	☐	☐	☐	☐
	☐	☐	☐	☐	☐	☐
	☐	☐	☐	☐	☐	☐
	☐	☐	☐	☐	☐	☐

Notes

September
Year 2021

"If people are doubting how far you can go, go so far that you can't hear them anymore"
-Michele Ruiz

Monthly And Daily Socially Relevant Holidays

Themes for the month of September:

- Childhood Cancer Awareness Month
- National Hispanic Heritage Month (September 15-October 15)

September 2021 hashtag calendar:

September 5 – International Day of Charity #CharityDay
September 6 – Read a Book Day #ReadABookDay
September 6 – Labor Day #LaborDay
September 8 – International Literacy Day #LiteracyDay
September 10 – Stand Up To Cancer Day #KissCancerGoodbye
September 11 – National Day of Service and Remembrance #911Day
September 12 – National Day of Encouragement #DayOfEncouragement
September 12 – National Video Games Day #NationalVideoGamesDay
September 12 – National Grandparents Day #NationalGrandparentsDay
September 14 – Live Creative Day #NationalLiveCreative Day #LiveCreativeDay
September 15 – Online Learning Day #OnlineLearningDay
September 19 – Talk Like a Pirate Day #TalkLikeAPirateDay
September 21 – International Day of Peace #PeaceDay
September 21 – Miniature Golf Day #MiniGolfDay
September 21 – Civic Day of Hacking #HackForChange

Monthly And Daily Socially Relevant Holiday

September 2021 hashtag calendar:

- September 21 – World Alzheimer's Day #Alzheimer'sDay
- September 22 – Car-Free Day #CarFreeDay
- September 22 – Hobbit Day #HobbitDay
- September 22 – First Day of Fall #1stDayOfFall
- September 26 – European Day of Languages #EDL2021
- September 27 – World Tourism Day #WTD2021
- September 28 – World Rabies Day #WorldRabiesDay
- September 28 – National Good Neighbor Day #GoodNeighborDay
- September 29 – International Coffee Day #InternationalCoffeeDay
- September 29 – National Women's Health and Fitness Day #FitnessDay
- September 30 – International Podcast Day #InternationalPodcastDay
- September 30 – National Love People Day #NationalLOVEPeopleDAY

Calender

Monday	Tuesday	Wednesday	Thursday	Friday	Saturday	Sunday
30	31	1	2	3	4	5
6	7	8	9	10	11	12
13	14	15	16	17	18	19
20	21	22	23	24	25	26
27	28	29	30	1	2	3

Notes

Content Strategy

Facebook
Account Name
Post Frequency
Content Ideas

Goals

Twitter
Account Name
Post Frequency
Content Ideas

Goals

Instagram
Account Name
Post Frequency
Content Ideas

Goals

Pinterest
Account Name
Post Frequency
Content Ideas

Goals

Media	No. of Subscribers	No. of Sales
Facebook		
Twitter		
Pinterest		
Instagram		

Blog Status

Notes

Monthly Paid Media Budget

Platform	Objective	Approved Budget

Total

Audience Details

Platform:

Notes

Total expenses

Post title _____ Month of _____

Day	Title	Category	Done

Notes

The Blog Post

PUBLISH DATE	CATEGORY	POST TYPE
POST TITLE		
RELATED SERIES		

BLOG NOTES

DESCRIPTION

- ......
- ......
- ......
- ......
- ......

KEY POINTS

- ......
- ......
- ......
- ......
- ......

INPUT LINKS

- ......
- ......
- ......

SOCIAL MEDIA

☐ f   ☐ 📷   ☐   ☐ P

OUTPUT LINKS

- ......
- ......
- ......

SPONSORS

GIVEAWAYS

FREEBIES

NOTES

The Blog Post

PUBLISH DATE	CATEGORY	POST TYPE
POST TITLE		
RELATED SERIES		

BLOG NOTES

DESCRIPTION

- [ ] ....
- [ ] ....
- [ ] ....
- [ ] ....
- [ ] ....

KEY POINTS

- [ ] ....
- [ ] ....
- [ ] ....
- [ ] ....
- [ ] ....

INPUT LINKS

- [ ] ....
- [ ] ....
- [ ] ....

SOCIAL MEDIA

- [ ] Facebook
- [ ] Instagram
- [ ] Pinterest

OUTPUT LINKS

- [ ] ....
- [ ] ....
- [ ] ....

SPONSORS

GIVEAWAYS

FREEBIES

NOTES

The Blog Post

PUBLISH DATE	CATEGORY	POST TYPE
POST TITLE		
RELATED SERIES		

BLOG NOTES

DESCRIPTION
- ....
- ....
- ....
- ....
- ....

KEY POINTS
- ....
- ....
- ....
- ....
- ....

INPUT LINKS
- ....
- ....
- ....

SOCIAL MEDIA
☐ f ☐ 📷 ☐ ☐ P

OUTPUT LINKS
- ....
- ....
- ....

SPONSORS

GIVEAWAYS

FREEBIES

NOTES

The Blog Post

PUBLISH DATE	CATEGORY	POST TYPE
POST TITLE		
RELATED SERIES		

Blog Notes

Description

-
-
-
-
-

Key Points

-
-
-
-
-

Input Links

-
-
-

Social Media

☐ f   ☐ 📷   ☐ p

Output Links

-
-
-

SPONSORS

GIVEAWAYS

FREEBIES

Notes

WEEK OF:

DATE:
BLOG TITLE:
IDEAS:

TAGS:
CATEGORIES:
KEYWORD PHRASE:
CALL TO ACTION:
AFFILIATE LINK TO PROMOTE:

TO DO:

POST PROMOTION:

WEEK OF:

DATE:
BLOG TITLE:
IDEAS:

TAGS:
CATEGORIES:
KEYWORD PHRASE:
CALL TO ACTION:
AFFILIATE LINK TO PROMOTE:

TO DO:

POST PROMOTION:

WEEK OF:

DATE:
BLOG TITLE:
IDEAS:

TAGS:
CATEGORIES:
KEYWORD PHRASE:
CALL TO ACTION:
AFFILIATE LINK TO PROMOTE:

TO DO:

POST PROMOTION:

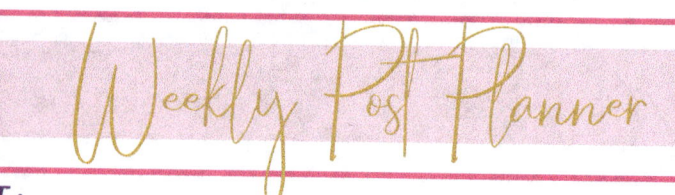

Weekly Post Planner

WEEK OF:

- DATE:
- BLOG TITLE:
- IDEAS:
- TAGS:
- CATEGORIES:
- KEYWORD PHRASE:
- CALL TO ACTION:
- AFFILIATE LINK TO PROMOTE:

TO DO:

POST PROMOTION:

WEEK OF:

- DATE:
- BLOG TITLE:
- IDEAS:
- TAGS:
- CATEGORIES:
- KEYWORD PHRASE:
- CALL TO ACTION:
- AFFILIATE LINK TO PROMOTE:

TO DO:

POST PROMOTION:

WEEK OF:

- DATE:
- BLOG TITLE:
- IDEAS:
- TAGS:
- CATEGORIES:
- KEYWORD PHRASE:
- CALL TO ACTION:
- AFFILIATE LINK TO PROMOTE:

TO DO:

POST PROMOTION:

Analytics

Total Users: ☐ New Users: ☐

Page Views ☐ Bounce Rate ☐

1 2 3 4 5 6 7 8 9 10 11 12

Pinterest Followers ☐ Pinterest Monthly Views ☐

Email Subscribers ☐ New Subscribers ☐

Instagram Followers ☐ Twitter Followers ☐

Facebook Page Likes ☐ Facebook Group Members ☐

Notes:

Community Management

Tasks

	M	T	W	T	F	S
	☐	☐	☐	☐	☐	☐
	☐	☐	☐	☐	☐	☐
	☐	☐	☐	☐	☐	☐
	☐	☐	☐	☐	☐	☐
	☐	☐	☐	☐	☐	☐
	☐	☐	☐	☐	☐	☐
	☐	☐	☐	☐	☐	☐
	☐	☐	☐	☐	☐	☐
	☐	☐	☐	☐	☐	☐
	☐	☐	☐	☐	☐	☐
	☐	☐	☐	☐	☐	☐
	☐	☐	☐	☐	☐	☐
	☐	☐	☐	☐	☐	☐

Notes

October
Year 2021

"There is no innovation and creativity without failure period."
-Brene brown

Monthly And Daily Socially Relevant Holidays

Themes for the month of October:

- Breast Cancer Awareness Month
- Domestic Violence Awareness Month
- Global Diversity Awareness Month
- National Bullying Prevention Awareness Month
- National Cyber Security Awareness Month

October 2021 hashtag calendar:

- October 1 – International Day of Older Persons #UNDOP
- October 1 – World Vegetarian Day #WorldVegetarianDay
- October 2 – Day of Nonviolence #InternationalDayOfNonviolence
- October 2 – National Techies Day #TechiesDay
- October 4 – World Animal Day #WorldAnimalDay
- October 4 – National Taco Day #NationalTacoDay
- October 4 – World Habitat Day #WorldHabitatDay
- October 5 – World Teachers Day #WorldTeachersDay
- October 10 – World Mental Health Day #WorldMentalHeathDay
- October 11 – International Day of the Girl #DayOfTheGirl
- October 13 – National Train Your Brain Day #TrainYourBrainDay
- October 14 – World Sight Day #WorldSightDay
- October 14 – National Dessert Day #DessertDay
- October 15 – Global Handwashing Day #GlobalHandwashingDay
- October 15 – Get to Know Your Customers Day #GetToKnowYourCustomersDay
- October 16 – National Boss's Day #NationalBossDay #BossDay #BestBossEver #HappyBossDay

Monthly And Daily Socially Relevant Holiday

October 2021 hashtag calendar:

- October 16 – World Food Day #FoodDay
- October 17 – National Clean Your Virtual Desktop Day #CleanYourVirtualDesktopDay
- October 17 – Eradication of Poverty Day #EndPoverty
- October 21 – Reptile Awareness Day #ReptileAwarenessDay
- October 24 – United Nations Day #UNDay
- October 25 – Greasy Foods Day #GreasyFoodsDay
- October 28 – National Chocolate Day #NationalChocolateDay
- October 30 – National Candy Corn Day #CandyCornDay
- October 30 – National Publicist Day #NationalPublicist
- October 31 – Halloween #Halloween

Calender

Monday	Tuesday	Wednesday	Thursday	Friday	Saturday	Sunday
27	28	29	30	1	2	3
4	5	6	7	8	9	10
11	12	13	14	15	16	17
18	19	20	21	22	23	24
25/31	26	27	28	29	30	31

Notes

www.theezeragency.com

Content Strategy

Facebook
Account Name
Post Frequency
Content Ideas

Goals

Twitter
Account Name
Post Frequency
Content Ideas

Goals

Instagram
Account Name
Post Frequency
Content Ideas

Goals

Pinterest
Account Name
Post Frequency
Content Ideas

Goals

Media	No. of Subscribers	No. of Sales
Facebook		
Twitter		
Pinterest		
Instagram		

Blog Status

Notes

Monthly Paid Media Budget

Platform	Objective	Approved Budget
Total		

Audience Details

Platform:

Notes

Total expenses

Blog Post Monthly

Post title _____ Month of _____

Day	Title	Category	Done

Notes

PUBLISH DATE	CATEGORY	POST TYPE
POST TITLE		
RELATED SERIES		

BLOG NOTES

DESCRIPTION

- ....
- ....
- ....
- ....
- ....

KEY POINTS

- ....
- ....
- ....
- ....
- ....

INPUT LINKS

- ....
- ....
- ....

SOCIAL MEDIA

☐ f ☐ 📷 ☐ ☐ p

OUTPUT LINKS

- ....
- ....
- ....

SPONSORS

GIVEAWAYS

FREEBIES

NOTES

The Blog Post

PUBLISH DATE	CATEGORY	POST TYPE
POST TITLE		
RELATED SERIES		

Blog Notes

Description

Key Points

Input Links

Social Media

SPONSORS

GIVEAWAYS

FREEBIES

Output Links

Notes

The Blog Post

PUBLISH DATE	CATEGORY	POST TYPE
POST TITLE		
RELATED SERIES		

BLOG NOTES

DESCRIPTION

- [ ]
- [ ]
- [ ]
- [ ]
- [ ]

KEY POINTS

- [ ]
- [ ]
- [ ]
- [ ]
- [ ]

INPUT LINKS

- [ ]
- [ ]
- [ ]

SOCIAL MEDIA

- [ ] f [ ] Instagram [ ] [ ] p

SPONSORS
GIVEAWAYS
FREEBIES

OUTPUT LINKS

- [ ]
- [ ]
- [ ]

NOTES

The Blog Post

PUBLISH DATE	CATEGORY	POST TYPE
POST TITLE		
RELATED SERIES		

BLOG NOTES

DESCRIPTION

KEY POINTS

INPUT LINKS

SOCIAL MEDIA
☐ f ☐ 📷 ☐ p

OUTPUT LINKS

SPONSORS

GIVEAWAYS

FREEBIES

NOTES

Weekly Post Planner

WEEK OF:

- DATE:
- BLOG TITLE:
- IDEAS:
- TAGS:
- CATEGORIES:
- KEYWORD PHRASE:
- CALL TO ACTION:
- AFFILIATE LINK TO PROMOTE:

TO DO:

POST PROMOTION:

WEEK OF:

- DATE:
- BLOG TITLE:
- IDEAS:
- TAGS:
- CATEGORIES:
- KEYWORD PHRASE:
- CALL TO ACTION:
- AFFILIATE LINK TO PROMOTE:

TO DO:

POST PROMOTION:

WEEK OF:

- DATE:
- BLOG TITLE:
- IDEAS:
- TAGS:
- CATEGORIES:
- KEYWORD PHRASE:
- CALL TO ACTION:
- AFFILIATE LINK TO PROMOTE:

TO DO:

POST PROMOTION:

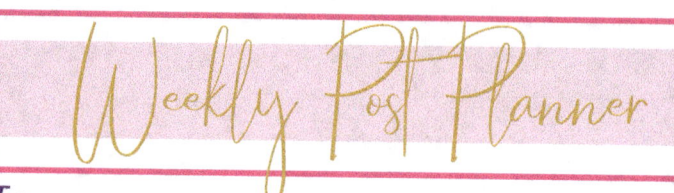

Weekly Post Planner

WEEK OF:

- DATE:
- BLOG TITLE:
- IDEAS:
- TAGS:
- CATEGORIES:
- KEYWORD PHRASE:
- CALL TO ACTION:
- AFFILIATE LINK TO PROMOTE:

TO DO:

POST PROMOTION:

WEEK OF:

- DATE:
- BLOG TITLE:
- IDEAS:
- TAGS:
- CATEGORIES:
- KEYWORD PHRASE:
- CALL TO ACTION:
- AFFILIATE LINK TO PROMOTE:

TO DO:

POST PROMOTION:

WEEK OF:

- DATE:
- BLOG TITLE:
- IDEAS:
- TAGS:
- CATEGORIES:
- KEYWORD PHRASE:
- CALL TO ACTION:
- AFFILIATE LINK TO PROMOTE:

TO DO:

POST PROMOTION:

Analytics

Total Users:

New Users:

Page Views

Bounce Rate

1 2 3 4 5 6 7 8 9 10 11 12

Pinterest Followers

Pinterest Monthly Views

Email Subscribers

New Subscribers

Instagram Followers

Twitter Followers

Facebook Page Likes

Facebook Group Members

Notes:

Community Management

Tasks	M	T	W	T	F	S
	☐	☐	☐	☐	☐	☐
	☐	☐	☐	☐	☐	☐
	☐	☐	☐	☐	☐	☐
	☐	☐	☐	☐	☐	☐
	☐	☐	☐	☐	☐	☐
	☐	☐	☐	☐	☐	☐
	☐	☐	☐	☐	☐	☐
	☐	☐	☐	☐	☐	☐
	☐	☐	☐	☐	☐	☐
	☐	☐	☐	☐	☐	☐
	☐	☐	☐	☐	☐	☐
	☐	☐	☐	☐	☐	☐

Notes

November
Year 2021

"Anything is possile if you've got enough nerve"
-J.K Rowling

Monthly And Daily Socially Relevant Holidays

Themes for the month of November:

- Novel Writing Month
- Epilepsy Awareness Month
- Men's Health Awareness Month

Weeks of observance in November:

- World Kindness Week: November 7-13
- Childrens' Book Week: November 8-14
- Random Acts of Kindness Week: November 15-22
- National Global Entrepreneurship Week: November 15-21
- Hanukkah: November 28 – December 6

Monthly And Daily Socially Relevant Holiday

November 2021 hashtag calendar:

- November 1 – World Vegan Day #WorldVeganDay
- November 1 – National Authors Day #NationalAuthorsDay
- November 3 – National Sandwich Day #NationalSandwichDay
- November 3 – International Stress Awareness Day #StressAwarenessDay
- November 4 – National Candy Day #NationalCandyDay
- November 7 – Daylight Saving Time Ends #DaylightSavings
- November 8 – National Cappuccino Day #CappuccinoDay
- November 8 – STEM Day #STEMDay
- November 11 – Veterans Day #VeteransDay
- November 13 – World Kindness Day #WKD
- November 14 – World Diabetes Day #WDD
- November 15 – Clean Out Your Refrigerator Day #CleanOutYourRefrigeratorDay
- November 15 – America Recycles Day #BeRecycled
- November 16 – International Day for Tolerance #ToleranceDay
- November 16 – National Entrepreneurs Day #EntrepreneursDay
- November 17 – International Students Day #InternationalStudentsDay
- November 19 – International Men's Day #InternationalMensDay
- November 19 – Women's Entrepreneurship Day #WomensEntrepreneurshipDay
- November 21 – World Day of Remembrance for Road Traffic Victims #WDoR2021 #WDoR
- November 21 – World Hello Day #WorldHelloDay
- November 25 – Thanksgiving Day #Thanksgiving
- November 26 – Black Friday #BlackFriday #BlackFriday2021
- November 26 – National Cake Day #NationalCakeDay
- November 26 – National Native American Heritage Day #NAHertitage #NativeAmericanHeritageDay
- November 27 – National Day of Listening #DayOfListening
- November 27 – Small Business Saturday #SmallBusinessSaturday
- November 29 – Cyber Monday #CyberMonday
- November 30 – Computer Security Day #ComputerSecurityDay
- November 30 – Giving Tuesday #GivingTuesday

Calender

Monday	Tuesday	Wednesday	Thursday	Friday	Saturday	Sunday
1	2	3	4	5	6	7
8	9	10	11	12	13	14
15	16	17	18	19	20	21
22	23	24	25	26	27	28
29	30	1	2	3	4	5

Notes

www.theezeragency.com

Content Strategy

Facebook

Account Name
....
Post Frequency
....
Content Ideas
....
....
Goals
....

Twitter

Account Name
....
Post Frequency
....
Content Ideas
....
....
Goals
....

Instagram

Account Name
....
Post Frequency
....
Content Ideas
....
....
Goals
....

Pinterest

Account Name
....
Post Frequency
....
Content Ideas
....
....
Goals
....

Media	No. of Subscribers	No. of Sales
Facebook		
Twitter		
Pinterest		
Instagram		

Blog Status

....
....
....
....

Notes

Monthly Paid Media Budget

Platform	Objective	Approved Budget
Total		

Audience Details

Platform:

Notes

Total expenses

Post title _____ Month of _____

Day	Title	Category	Done

Notes

PUBLISH DATE	CATEGORY	POST TYPE
POST TITLE		
RELATED SERIES		

BLOG NOTES

DESCRIPTION

- ....
- ....
- ....
- ....
- ....

KEY POINTS

- ....
- ....
- ....
- ....
- ....

INPUT LINKS

- ....
- ....
- ....

SOCIAL MEDIA

☐ f ☐ ⊙ ☐ ☐ p

OUTPUT LINKS

- ....
- ....
- ....

SPONSORS

GIVEAWAYS

FREEBIES

NOTES

The Blog Post

PUBLISH DATE	CATEGORY	POST TYPE
POST TITLE		
RELATED SERIES		

BLOG NOTES

DESCRIPTION

- ....
- ....
- ....
- ....
- ....

KEY POINTS

- ....
- ....
- ....
- ....
- ....

INPUT LINKS

- ....
- ....
- ....

SOCIAL MEDIA

☐ f   ☐ 📷   ☐ p

OUTPUT LINKS

- ....
- ....
- ....

SPONSORS

GIVEAWAYS

FREEBIES

NOTES

PUBLISH DATE	CATEGORY	POST TYPE
POST TITLE		
RELATED SERIES		

BLOG NOTES

DESCRIPTION

KEY POINTS

INPUT LINKS

SOCIAL MEDIA

OUTPUT LINKS

SPONSORS

GIVEAWAYS

FREEBIES

NOTES

The Blog Post

PUBLISH DATE	CATEGORY	POST TYPE
POST TITLE		
RELATED SERIES		

BLOG NOTES

DESCRIPTION

- ....
- ....
- ....
- ....
- ....

KEY POINTS

- ....
- ....
- ....
- ....
- ....

INPUT LINKS

- ....
- ....
- ....

SOCIAL MEDIA

☐ f   ☐ ⊙   ☐ p

SPONSORS

GIVEAWAYS

FREEBIES

OUTPUT LINKS

- ....
- ....
- ....

NOTES

Weekly Post Planner

WEEK OF:

- DATE:
- BLOG TITLE:
- IDEAS:
- TAGS:
- CATEGORIES:
- KEYWORD PHRASE:
- CALL TO ACTION:
- AFFILIATE LINK TO PROMOTE:

TO DO:

POST PROMOTION:

WEEK OF:

- DATE:
- BLOG TITLE:
- IDEAS:
- TAGS:
- CATEGORIES:
- KEYWORD PHRASE:
- CALL TO ACTION:
- AFFILIATE LINK TO PROMOTE:

TO DO:

POST PROMOTION:

WEEK OF:

- DATE:
- BLOG TITLE:
- IDEAS:
- TAGS:
- CATEGORIES:
- KEYWORD PHRASE:
- CALL TO ACTION:
- AFFILIATE LINK TO PROMOTE:

TO DO:

POST PROMOTION:

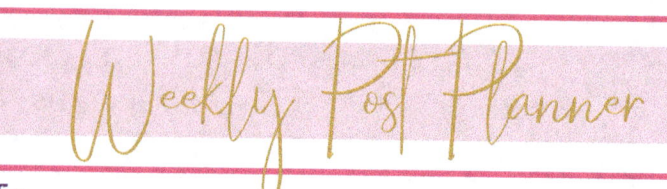

Weekly Post Planner

WEEK OF:

- DATE:
- BLOG TITLE:
- IDEAS:
- TAGS:
- CATEGORIES:
- KEYWORD PHRASE:
- CALL TO ACTION:
- AFFILIATE LINK TO PROMOTE:

TO DO:

POST PROMOTION:

WEEK OF:

- DATE:
- BLOG TITLE:
- IDEAS:
- TAGS:
- CATEGORIES:
- KEYWORD PHRASE:
- CALL TO ACTION:
- AFFILIATE LINK TO PROMOTE:

TO DO:

POST PROMOTION:

WEEK OF:

- DATE:
- BLOG TITLE:
- IDEAS:
- TAGS:
- CATEGORIES:
- KEYWORD PHRASE:
- CALL TO ACTION:
- AFFILIATE LINK TO PROMOTE:

TO DO:

POST PROMOTION:

Analytics

Total Users: New Users:

Page Views Bounce Rate

1 2 3 4 5 6 7 8 9 10 11 12

Pinterest Followers   Pinterest Monthly Views

Email Subscribers   New Subscribers

Instagram Followers   Twitter Followers

Facebook Page Likes   Facebook Group Members

Notes:

Community Management

Tasks

M T W T F S

Notes

December

Year 2021

"If you're serious about changing your life, you'll find a way. If you're not, you'll find an excuse."
-Jen Sincero

Monthly And Daily Socially Relevant Holidays

Themes for the month of December:

AIDS Awareness Month

Weeks of observance in December:

Hanukkah: November 28 – December 6
Human Rights Week: December 10-17
Kwanzaa: December 26 – January 1

December 2021 hashtag calendar:

- December 1 – World AIDS Day #WAD2020
- December 3 – Persons with Disabilities Day #IDPWD
- December 4 – National Cookie Day #NationalCookieDay
- December 5 – World Soil Day #WorldSoilDay
- December 8 – Pretend to Be a Time Traveler Day #PretendToBeATimeTravelerDay
- December 10 – Human Rights Day #HumanRightsDay
- December 10 – Nobel Prize Day #NobelPrize
- December 11 – International Mountain Day #InternationalMountainDay
- December 21 – Crossword Puzzle Day #CrosswordPuzzleDay
- December 21 – First Day of Winter #WinterSolstice
- December 25 – Christmas Day #Christmas
- December 27 – No Interruptions Day #NoInterruptionsDay
- December 31 – New Year's Eve #NewYearsEve

Calender

Monday	Tuesday	Wednesday	Thursday	Friday	Saturday	Sunday
29	30	1	2	3	4	5
6	7	8	9	10	11	12
13	14	15	16	17	18	19
20	21	22	23	24	25	26
27	28	29	30	31	1	2

Notes

www.theezeragency.com

Content Strategy

Facebook

Account Name
....
Post Frequency
....
Content Ideas
....
....
Goals
....

Twitter

Account Name
....
Post Frequency
....
Content Ideas
....
....
Goals
....

Instagram

Account Name
....
Post Frequency
....
Content Ideas
....
....
Goals
....

Pinterest

Account Name
....
Post Frequency
....
Content Ideas
....
....
Goals
....

Media	No. of Subscribers	No. of Sales
Facebook		
Twitter		
Pinterest		
Instagram		

Blog Status

....
....
....
....

Notes

Monthly Paid Media Budget

Platform	Objective	Approved Budget
Total		

Audience Details

Platform:

Total expenses

Notes

Post title _____ **Month of** _____

Day	Title	Category	Done

Notes

The Blog Post

PUBLISH DATE	CATEGORY	POST TYPE
POST TITLE		
RELATED SERIES		

BLOG NOTES

DESCRIPTION

-
-
-
-
-
-

KEY POINTS

-
-
-
-
-

INPUT LINKS

-
-
-
-

SOCIAL MEDIA

☐ f   ☐ ⊙   ☐   ☐ ℘

OUTPUT LINKS

-
-
-

SPONSORS

GIVEAWAYS

FREEBIES

NOTES

The Blog Post

PUBLISH DATE	CATEGORY	POST TYPE
POST TITLE		
RELATED SERIES		

BLOG NOTES

DESCRIPTION

- ....
- ....
- ....
- ....
- ....

KEY POINTS

- ....
- ....
- ....
- ....
- ....

INPUT LINKS

- ....
- ....
- ....

SOCIAL MEDIA

☐ f   ☐ ⊙   ☐ p

OUTPUT LINKS

- ....
- ....
- ....

SPONSORS

GIVEAWAYS

FREEBIES

NOTES

The Blog Post

PUBLISH DATE	CATEGORY	POST TYPE
POST TITLE		
RELATED SERIES		

Blog Notes

Description
-
-
-
-
-

Key Points
-
-
-
-
-

Input Links
-
-
-

Social Media
☐ f ☐ 📷 ☐ p

Output Links
-
-
-

SPONSORS

GIVEAWAYS

FREEBIES

Notes

The Blog Post

PUBLISH DATE	CATEGORY	POST TYPE
POST TITLE		
RELATED SERIES		

BLOG NOTES

DESCRIPTION

- ....
- ....
- ....
- ....
- ....

KEY POINTS

- ....
- ....
- ....
- ....
- ....

INPUT LINKS

- ....
- ....
- ....

SOCIAL MEDIA

☐ f ☐ 📷 ☐ ☐ P

OUTPUT LINKS

- ....
- ....
- ....

SPONSORS

GIVEAWAYS

FREEBIES

NOTES

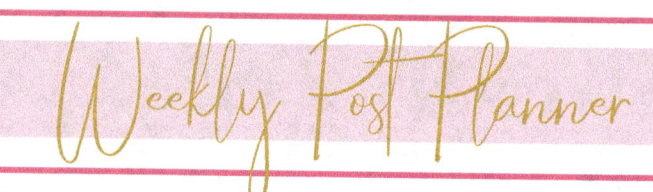

Weekly Post Planner

WEEK OF:

- DATE:
- BLOG TITLE:
- IDEAS:
- TAGS:
- CATEGORIES:
- KEYWORD PHRASE:
- CALL TO ACTION:
- AFFILIATE LINK TO PROMOTE:

TO DO:

POST PROMOTION:

WEEK OF:

- DATE:
- BLOG TITLE:
- IDEAS:
- TAGS:
- CATEGORIES:
- KEYWORD PHRASE:
- CALL TO ACTION:
- AFFILIATE LINK TO PROMOTE:

TO DO:

POST PROMOTION:

WEEK OF:

- DATE:
- BLOG TITLE:
- IDEAS:
- TAGS:
- CATEGORIES:
- KEYWORD PHRASE:
- CALL TO ACTION:
- AFFILIATE LINK TO PROMOTE:

TO DO:

POST PROMOTION:

Weekly Post Planner

WEEK OF:

- DATE:
- BLOG TITLE:
- IDEAS:
- TAGS:
- CATEGORIES:
- KEYWORD PHRASE:
- CALL TO ACTION:
- AFFILIATE LINK TO PROMOTE:

TO DO:

POST PROMOTION:

WEEK OF:

- DATE:
- BLOG TITLE:
- IDEAS:
- TAGS:
- CATEGORIES:
- KEYWORD PHRASE:
- CALL TO ACTION:
- AFFILIATE LINK TO PROMOTE:

TO DO:

POST PROMOTION:

WEEK OF:

- DATE:
- BLOG TITLE:
- IDEAS:
- TAGS:
- CATEGORIES:
- KEYWORD PHRASE:
- CALL TO ACTION:
- AFFILIATE LINK TO PROMOTE:

TO DO:

POST PROMOTION:

Analytics

Total Users: ☐   New Users: ☐

Page Views ☐   Bounce Rate ☐

1	2	3	4	5	6	7	8	9	10	11	12

Pinterest Followers ☐   Pinterest Monthly Views ☐

Email Subscribers ☐   New Subscribers ☐

Instagram Followers ☐   Twitter Followers ☐

Facebook Page Likes ☐   Facebook Group Members ☐

Notes:

Community Management

Tasks

	M	T	W	T	F	S
	☐	☐	☐	☐	☐	☐
	☐	☐	☐	☐	☐	☐
	☐	☐	☐	☐	☐	☐
	☐	☐	☐	☐	☐	☐
	☐	☐	☐	☐	☐	☐
	☐	☐	☐	☐	☐	☐
	☐	☐	☐	☐	☐	☐
	☐	☐	☐	☐	☐	☐
	☐	☐	☐	☐	☐	☐
	☐	☐	☐	☐	☐	☐
	☐	☐	☐	☐	☐	☐
	☐	☐	☐	☐	☐	☐

Notes

Checklist

Date

Name

Things To Do	Action Date

Important Notes

Daily Tasks

To-do list:

- [ ]
- [ ]
- [ ]
- [ ]
- [ ]
- [ ]
- [ ]

Notes:

6:00 AM
6:30 AM
7:00 AM
7:30 AM
8:00 AM
8:30 AM
9:00 AM
9:30 AM
10:00 AM
10:30 AM
11:00 AM
11:30 AM
12:00 PM
12:30 PM
1:00 PM
1:30 PM
2:00 PM
2:30 PM
3:00 PM
3:30 PM
4:00 PM
4:30 PM
5:00 PM

Task List

WEEK 01

WEEK 02

WEEK 03

WEEK 04

WEEK 05

WEEK 06

WEEK 07

Task Schedule

Name:

Position:

Target:

Date	Tasks	Start	End

Post Title _____ **Date** _____

Post Type _____ **Category** _____

Guidelines
....
....
....
....

Keypoints
....
....
....
....

Images
....
....
....
....

Tags & Keywords
....
....
....
....

Share On
Facebook ....
Twitter ....
Pinterest ....
Instagram ....

Links
....
....
....
....

No. Of Views	No. Of Comments
....	....
....	....
....	....

TO DO

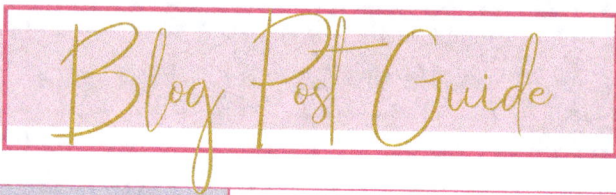

Blog Post Guide

What is your topic
Write down the main idea or theme you want to write about

Who is your audience
How knowledgeable is your target audience

When to post
When do you plan to publish the post?

What post types/structure
How do you plan to organize the post?

Reason for post
Why do you feel this post is important for your readers?

Notes:

To do:

My Daily Planner For Achieving My Goals

Date _____

My Top 3 Priorities

1.	2.	3.

People I must Reach Out Today

1.	2.	3.

Takes that must be completed before end of the day

1.	2.	3.

Schedule the above items into my day below

My Day

- 6 AM
- 7 AM
- 8 AM
- 9 AM
- 10 AM
- 11 AM
- 12 PM
- 1 PM
- 2 PM
- 3 PM
- 4 PM
- 5 PM
- 6 PM
- 7 PM
- 8 PM
- 9 PM
- 10 PM

Today's Treat

I'm Grateful For
1.
2.
3.

Notes

Monthly Goal

Date		Month	
week 1	**week 2**	**week 3**	**week 4**

Week 5

Top Goals

This Month's Focus

Meeting Planner

| Month | 1 Jan | 2 Feb | 3 Mar | 4 Apr | 5 May | 6 Jun | 7 Jul | 8 Aug | 9 Sep | 10 Oct | 11 Nov | 12 Dec | Year |

Notes
....
....
....
....
....

Description
....
....
....
....
....

Meetings	Events	Type	Estimated date	Start Date	Finish Date

Notes
....
....
....

To Do List
....
....
....
....
....
....

Reminders
....
....
....

Financial Planner

Month 1 Jan 2 Feb 3 Mar 4 Apr 5 May 6 Jun 7 Jul 8 Aug 9 Sep 10 Oct 11 Nov 12 Dec **Year**

PRODUCT/SERVICE	BILL PAYMENT	PRICE

Resources

....
....
....

Savings

Important Matters

	Events	Type	Estimated date	Start Date	Finish Date
Meetings					

Month   1   2   3   4   5   6   7   8   9   10   11   12   **Year**
        Jan Feb Mar Apr May Jun Jul Aug Sep Oct Nov Dec

Top Goals

Strategy

Action Steps

Notes

....
....
....
....

Reminder

....
....
....
....

Date　Mon　Tue　Wed　Thurs　Fri　Sat　Sun

Project/Goals

Routine

To Do List

Task Tracker

Notes

Time Management

Month   1   2   3   4   5   6   7   8   9   10   11   12   **Year**
         Jan   Feb   Mar   Apr   May   Jun   Jul   Aug   Sep   Oct   Nov   Dec

Appointments

Mon

Tue

Wed

Thurs

Fri

Sat

Sun

Task Tracker

Notes

Daily Planner

Date _____

Monday
Tasks & Appointments

Tasks & Appointments

Tuesday
Tasks & Appointments

Wednesday
Tasks & Appointments

Thursday
Tasks & Appointments

Friday
Tasks & Appointments

Saturday
Tasks & Appointments

Sunday
Tasks & Appointments

MONTH _____   **YEAR** _____

Appointments

Mon

Tue

Wed

Thurs

Fri

Sat

Sun

Task

Notes

Two Week Plan

Month 1 Jan 2 Feb 3 Mar 4 Apr 5 May 6 Jun 7 Jul 8 Aug 9 Sep 10 Oct 11 Nov 12 Dec **Year**

Appointments

Tasks

Mon	Mon
Tue	Tue
Wed	Wed
Thurs	Thurs
Fri	Fri
Sat	Sat
Sun	Sun

Reminders

Notes

www.ingramcontent.com/pod-product-compliance
Lightning Source LLC
Chambersburg PA
CBHW052032300426
44117CB00012B/1791